The Joy of Flute

MW01013879

**Edited by Jerome Goldstein with simple piano
arrangements by Denes Agay.**

The Joy of Flute is a colourful, well-balanced repertoire of appealing solo pieces,
with piano accompaniment, designed for the beginning and intermediate grade player. Here are familiar themes
by the masters, classic and modern, folk tunes, favourite standard songs and popular melodies of today.
The variety is both pleasing and educational.

In general, the selection follows a graded sequence. The first few pieces can be played as early as the
second or third month of study. The shorter selections may be combined into groups of two or three, and
are playable in sequence to form a longer, more impressive recital unit. A few suggestions as to
such groupings may be found below.

This collection was expertly edited by Jerome Goldstein, former member of the Pittsburgh and Dallas
Symphonies, presently a well-known band director and educator. The piano accompaniments,
always simple and well-sounding, are by Denes Agay, whose work in the field of piano teaching materials
is widely known and respected.

The Joy of Flute is an excellent supplement and companion book to any good flute method.
It provides carefully selected, enjoyable pieces for the technical and musical development of the young player.

Here are a few examples for effective grouping of the shorter selections:

Down In The Valley	**The Trout**
Red River Valley	**Chit-Chat**
Lament	**Melody**
Maypole Dance	**Comedians' Galop**
The Lonesome Road	**Theme from 'Pathétique Symphony'**
When The Saints Go Marching In	**Capriccio Italien**
Vilia	**Aria from 'Don Giovanni'**
Rumanian Rhapsody	**Rondino**
Sarabande	**Aura Lee**
Bourrée	**Roses From The South**
Blow The Man Down	**Finale from Symphony No.1**
House Of The Rising Sun	**German Dance**
Folk Boogie	**The Bagpipers**

Exclusive Distributors:
Music Sales Limited
8/9 Frith Street, London W1V 5TZ, England.
Music Sales Pty Limited
120 Rothschild Avenue, Rosebery, NSW 2018, Australia.

This book © Copyright 1993 by
Yorktown Music Press/Music Sales Limited
Order No.YK21616
ISBN 0-7119-3169-0

Cover illustration by Paul Leith
Compiled by Peter Evans
Music arranged by Cyril Ornadel
Music processed by Seton Music Graphics

Music Sales' complete catalogue lists thousands of titles and is
free from your local music shop, or direct from Music Sales Limited.
Please send a cheque/postal order for £1.50 for postage to:
Music Sales Limited, Newmarket Road, Bury St. Edmunds, Suffolk IP33 3YB.

Your Guarantee of Quality

As publishers, we strive to produce every book to the
highest commercial standards.

The music has been freshly engraved and the book has been carefully designed
to minimise awkward page turns and to make playing from it a real pleasure.

Particular care has been given to specifying acid-free, neutral-sized
paper which has not been chlorine bleached but produced with
special regard for the environment.
Throughout, the printing and binding have been planned to ensure a sturdy,
attractive publication which should give years of enjoyment.

If your copy fails to meet our high standards, please inform us and
we will gladly replace it.

Printed in the United Kingdom by
J.B. Offset Printers (Marks Tey) Limited, Marks Tey, Essex.

Yorktown Music Press / Music Sales Limited
London / New York / Paris / Sydney / Copenhagen / Madrid

CONTENTS

1. The Carman's Whistle

Composed by William Byrd

2. Down In The Valley

Folk Song

3. Red River Valley

Cowboy Song

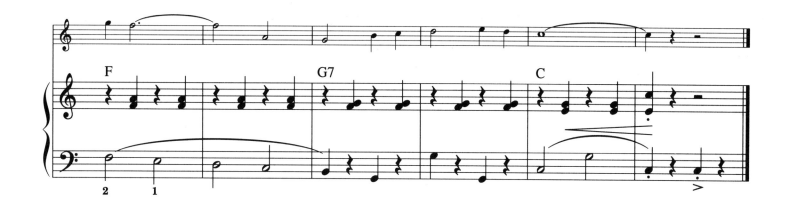

4. Blow The Man Down

Sea Shanty

5. Folk Boogie

6. House Of The Rising Sun

Folk Ballad

7. The Riddle Song

Folk Song

8. Roses From The South

Composed by Johann Strauss

9. Lament

Composed by Béla Bartók

10. Maypole Dance

Composed by Béla Bartók

11. Give My Regards To Broadway

Words & Music by George M. Cohan

12. The Lonesome Road

Words by Gene Austin. Music by Nathaniel Shilkret

13. We Three Kings Of Orient Are

Composed by John Henry Hopkins Jr..

14. Plaisir d'Amour

Composed by Giovanni Paolo Martini

15. When The Saints Go Marching In

Traditional

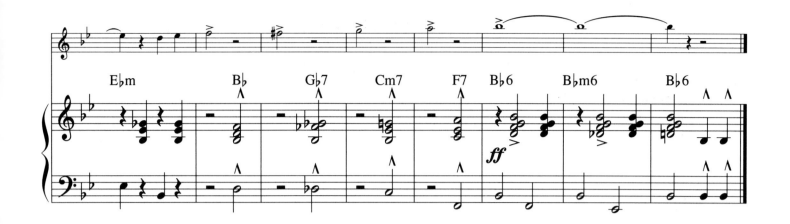

16. Aura Lee

Composed by George R. Pulton

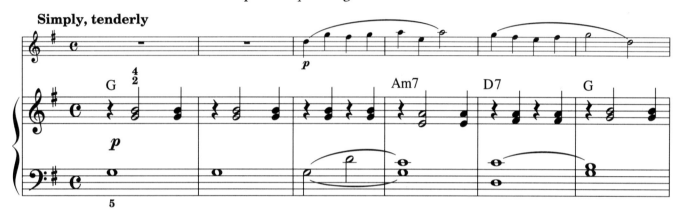

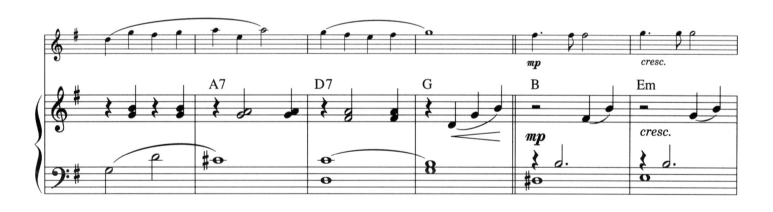

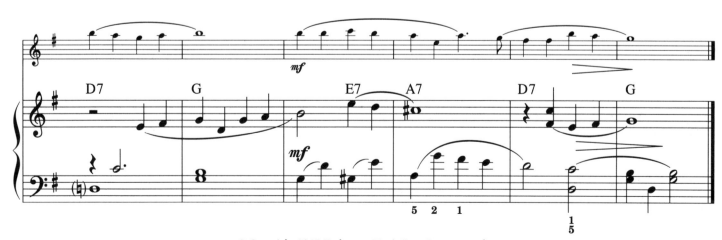

17. Chit-Chat

Composed by Dmitri Kabalevsky

18. Marian

Calypso Song

19. The Bagpipers (Theme from Symphony No. 104)

Composed by Joseph Haydn

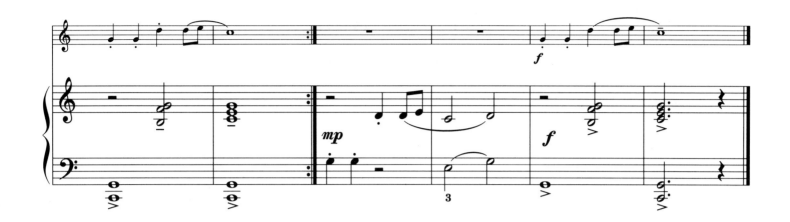

20. German Dance

Composed by Ludwig Van Beethoven

Allegretto

21. The Trout

Composed by Franz Schubert

22. Melody

Composed by Robert Schumann

23. Vilia (Vilja)

Music by Franz Lehár

24. Rumanian Rhapsody

Composed by Georges Enesco

25. Comedians' Galop

Composed by Dmitri Kabalevsky

26. Black Is The Colour Of My True Love's Hair

Folk Song

27. Sarabande

Composed by Arcangelo Corelli

28. Bourrée

Composed by Johann Krieger

29. Aria From Don Giovanni (La Ci Darem La Mano)

Composed by Wolfgang Amadeus Mozart

The Joy of Flute

Edited by Jerome Goldstein with simple piano arrangements by Denes Agay.

CONTENTS

Yorktown Music Press / Music Sales Limited
London / New York / Paris / Sydney / Copenhagen / Madrid

1. The Carman's Whistle

Composed by William Byrd

2. Down In The Valley

Folk Song

3. Red River Valley

Cowboy Song

4. Blow The Man Down

Sea Shanty

5. Folk Boogie

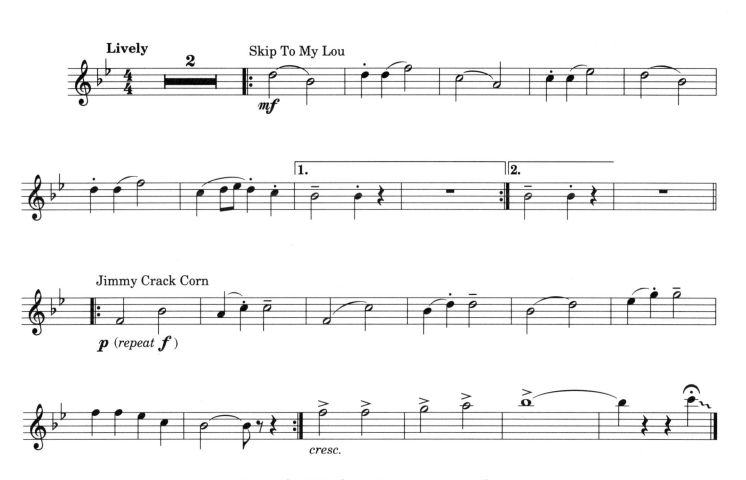

3

6. House Of The Rising Sun

Folk Ballad

7. The Riddle Song

Folk Song

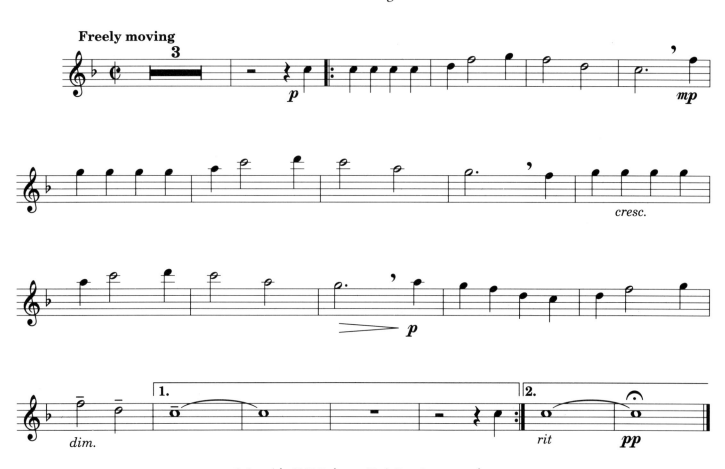

4

8. Roses From The South

Composed by Johann Strauss

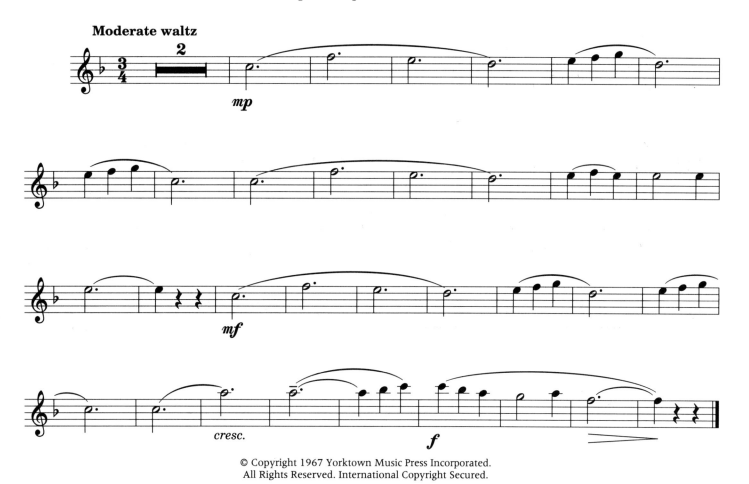

9. Lament

Composed by Béla Bartók

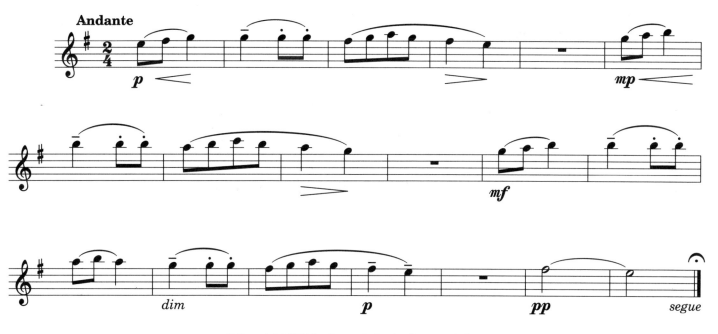

10. Maypole Dance

Composed by Béla Bartók

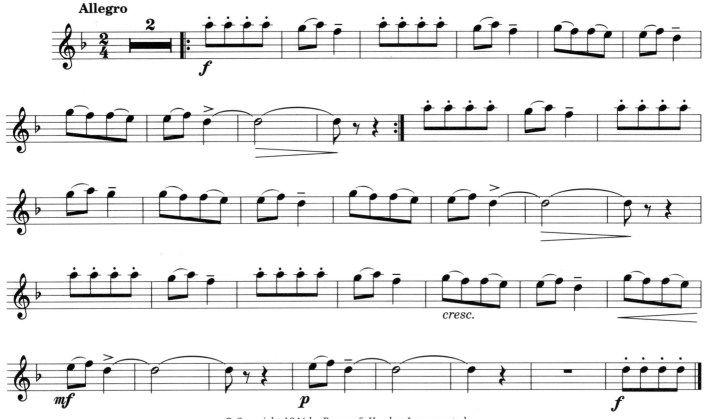

11. Give My Regards To Broadway

Words & Music by George M. Cohan

12. The Lonesome Road

Words by Gene Austin. Music by Nathaniel Shilkret

13. We Three Kings Of Orient Are

Composed by John Henry Hopkins Jr.

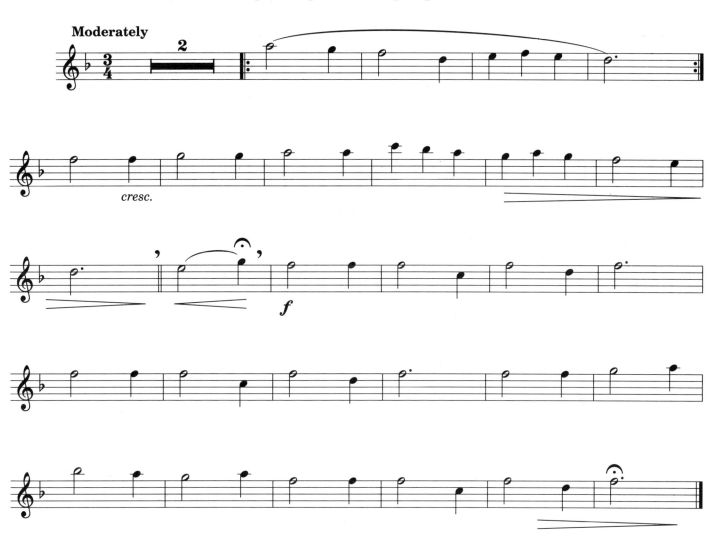

14. Plaisir d'Amour

Composed by Giovanni Paolo Martini

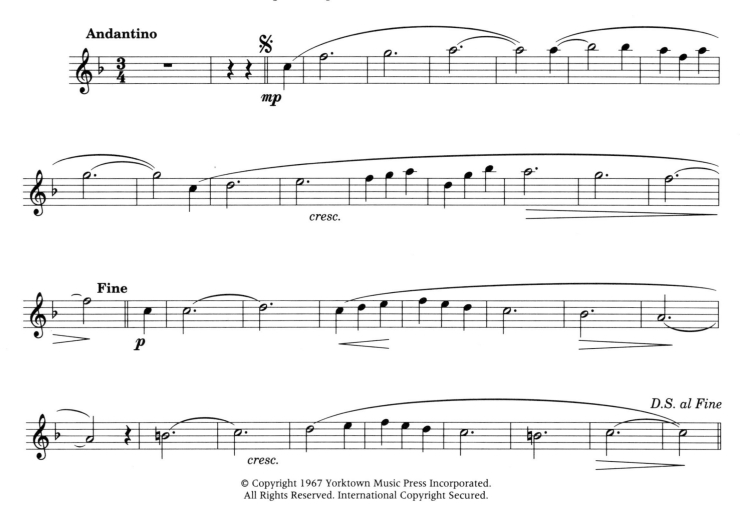

15. When The Saints Go Marching In

Traditional

16. Aura Lee

Composed by George R. Pulton

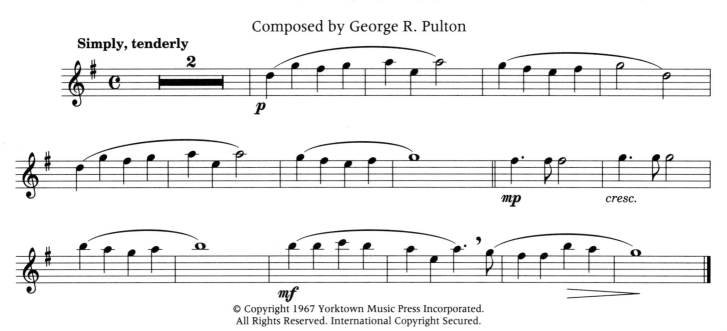

17. Chit-Chat

Composed by Dmitri Kabalevsky

18. Marian

Calypso Song

19. The Bagpipers (Theme from Symphony No. 104)

Composed by Joseph Haydn

20. German Dance

Composed by Ludwig Van Beethoven

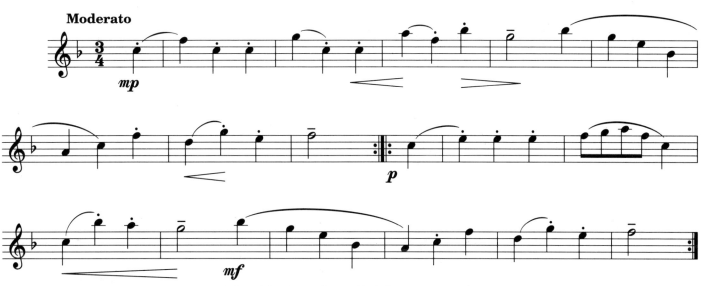

21. The Trout

Franz Schubert

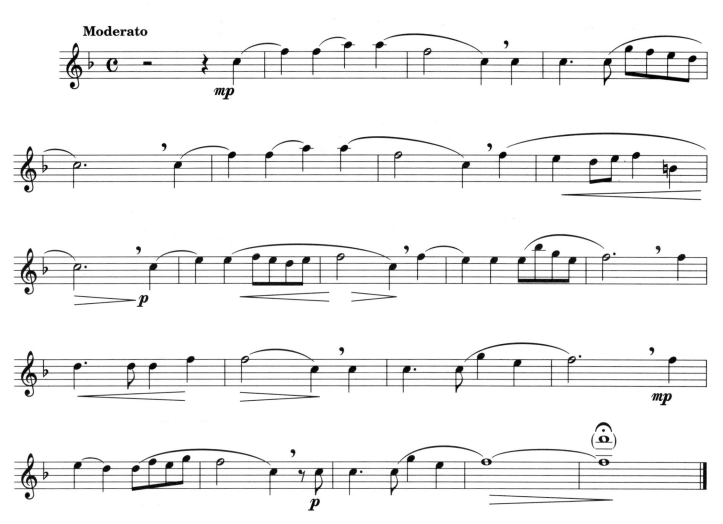

11

22. Melody

Composed by Robert Schumann

23. Vilia (Vilja)

Music by Franz Lehár

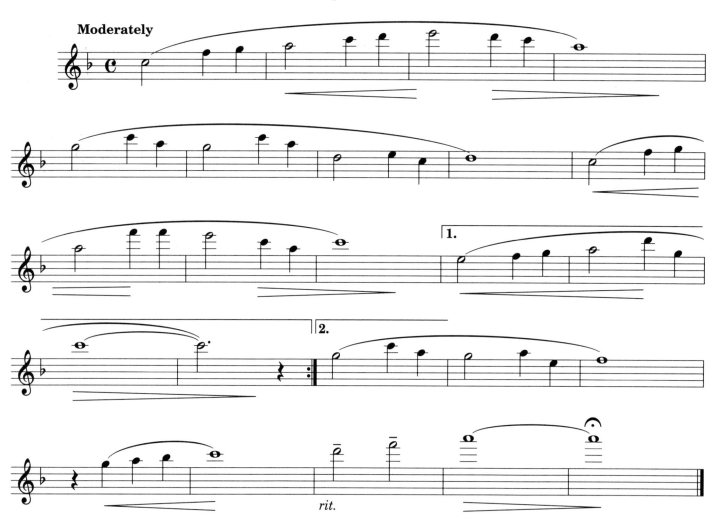

24. Rumanian Rhapsody

Composed by Georges Enesco

25. Comedians' Galop

Composed by Dmitri Kabalevsky

D.C. al Fine

26. Black Is The Colour Of My True Love's Hair

Folk Song

27. Sarabande

Composed by Arcangelo Corelli

28. Bourrée

Composed by Johann Krieger

29. Aria From Don Giovanni (La Ci Darem La Mano)

Composed by Wolfgang Amadeus Mozart

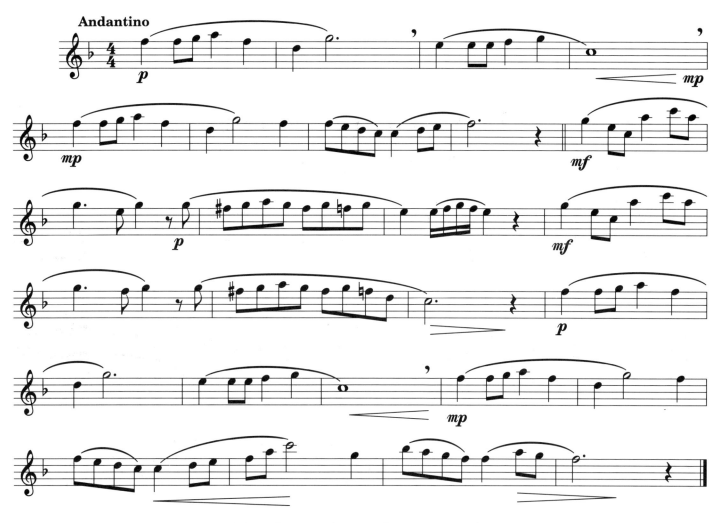

30. Theme From Pathétique Symphony

Composed by Peter Ilyich Tchaikovsky

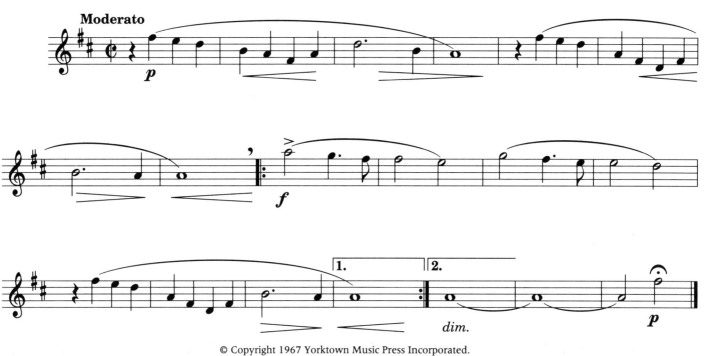

31. Venetian Boat Song

Composed by Felix Mendelssohn

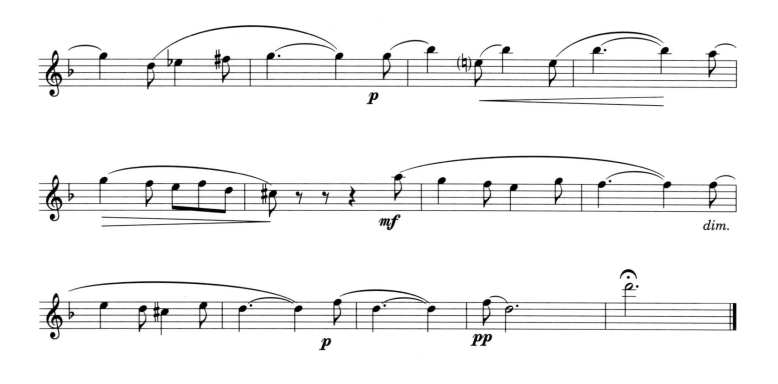

32. Finale From Symphony No.1

Composed by Johannes Brahms

33. Capriccio Italien

Composed by Peter Ilyich Tchaikovsky

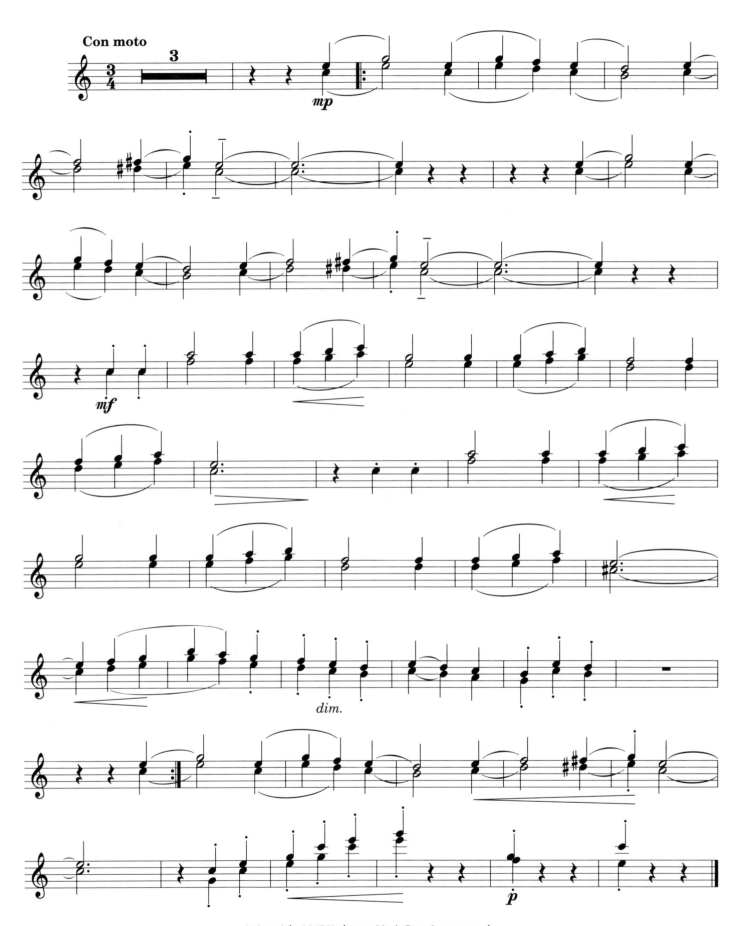

34. Gypsy Life

Composed by V. Monti

35. Romance (from The Pearl Fishers)

Composed by Georges Bizet

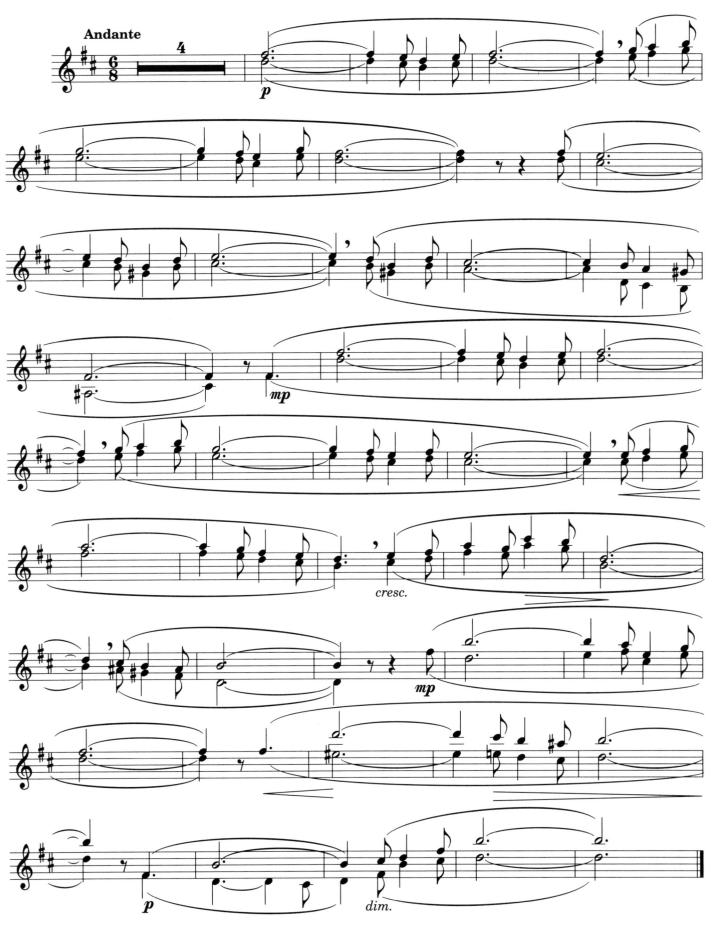

36. Variations on Little Brown Jug

Composed by Gerald Martin

37. Musette

Composed by Johann Sebastian Bach

Andante pastorale

38. Nocturne

Composed by Frédéric Chopin

Andante

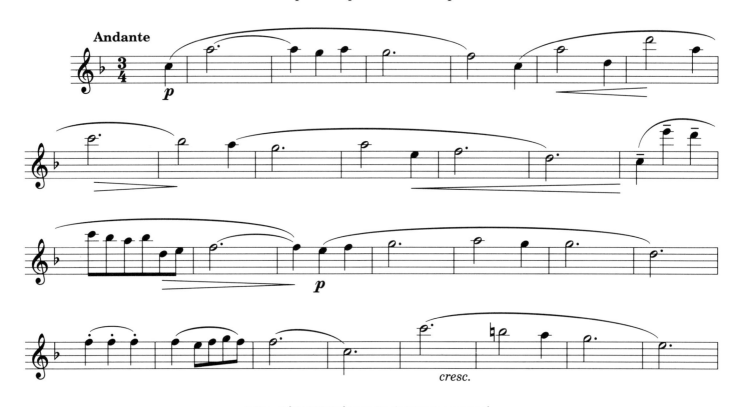

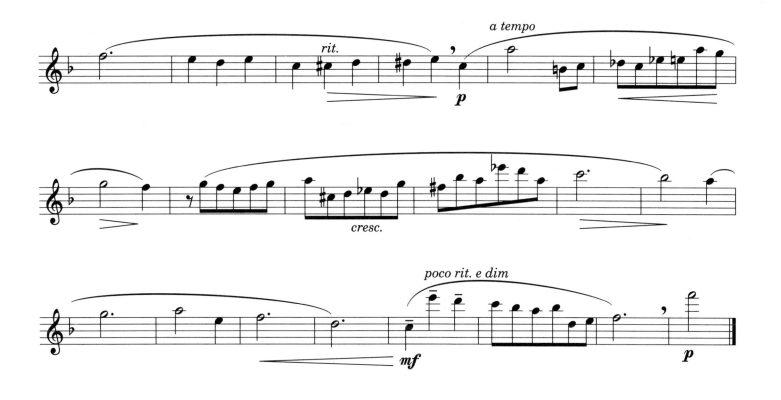

39. A Touch Of Blues

Composed by Gerald Martin

40. Rondino (Theme from Divertimento No. 14)

Composed by Wolfgang Amadeus Mozart

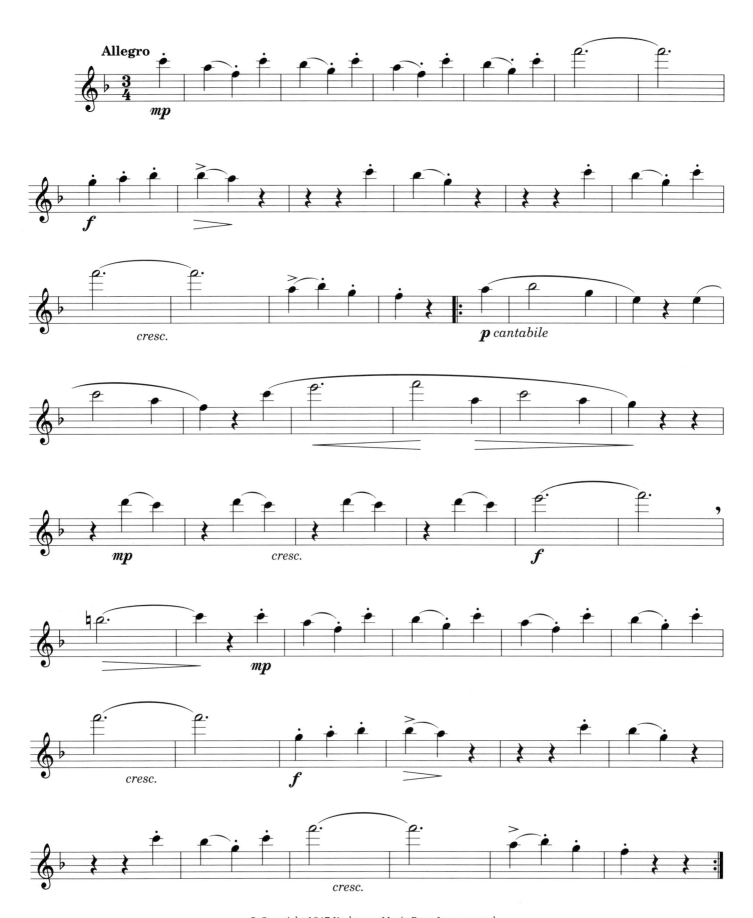

3/94　(17412)

30. Theme From Pathétique Symphony

Composed by Peter Ilyich Tchaikovsky

31. Venetian Boat Song

Composed by Felix Mendelssohn

32. Finale From Symphony No.1

Composed by Johannes Brahms

33. Capriccio Italien

Composed by Peter Ilyich Tchaikovsky

34. Gypsy Life

Composed by V. Monti

35. Romance (from The Pearl Fishers)

Composed by Georges Bizet

36. Variations on Little Brown Jug

Composed by Gerald Martin

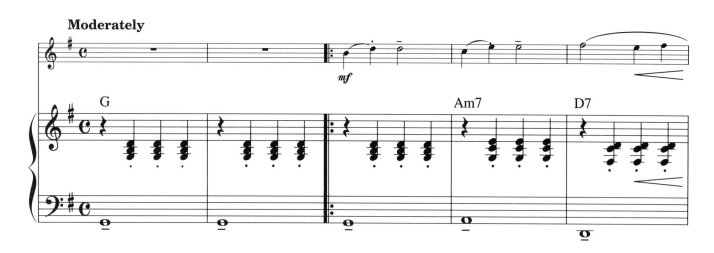

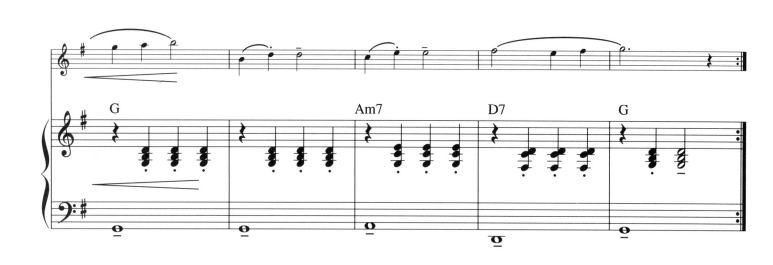

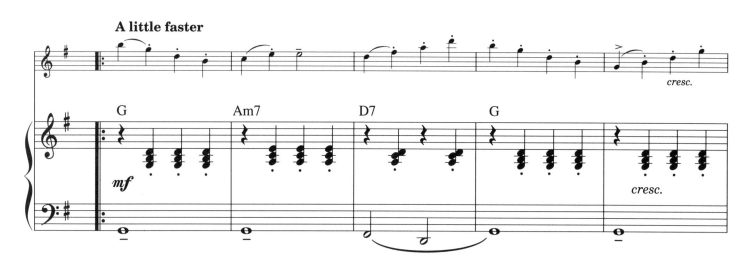

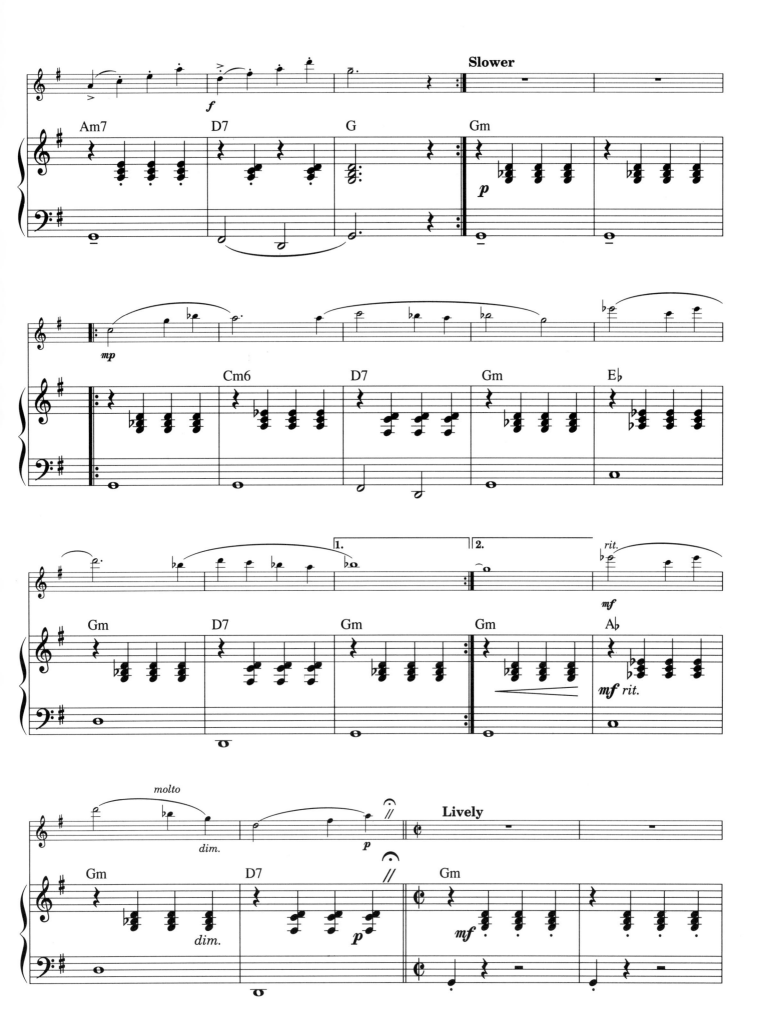

37. Musette

Composed by Johann Sebastian Bach

38. Nocturne

Composed by Frédéric Chopin

39. A Touch Of Blues

Composed by Gerald Martin

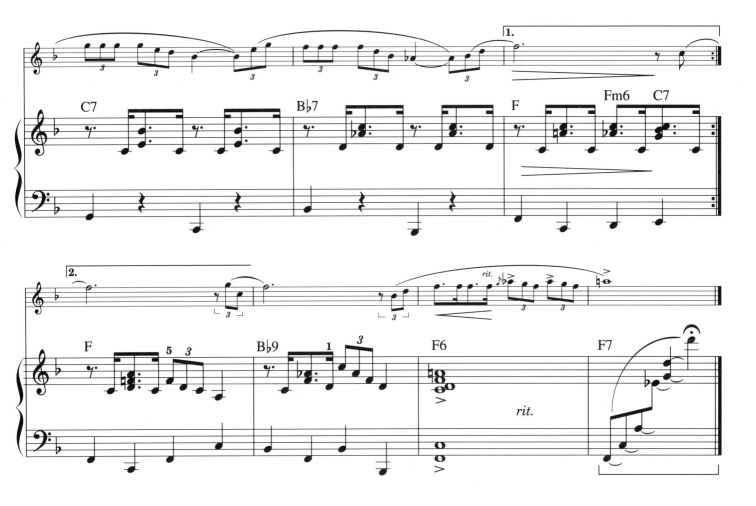

40. Rondino (Theme from Divertimento No. 14)

Composed by Wolfgang Amadeus Mozart

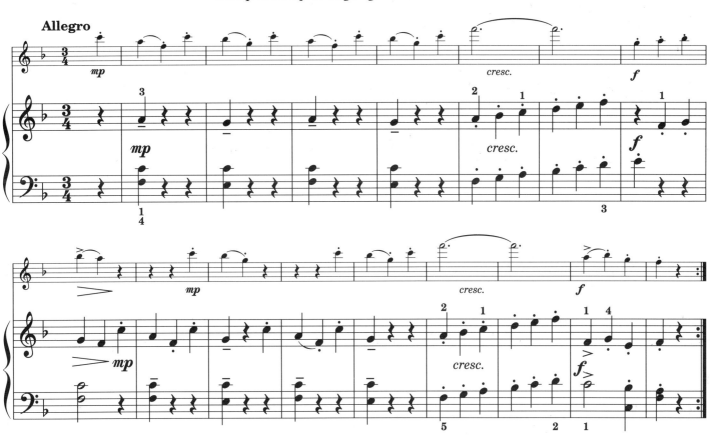

3/94 (17412)